I0390995

POLYPHONIC (AUTO)BIOGRAPHY SYNDROME

POLYPHONIC (AUTO)BIOGRAPHY SYNDROME

Weronika Trojanska / Sandberg Instituut, 2015

First Printing: 2015

ISBN 978-1-326-15186-7

CONTENTS

ally, we may, mimicking Dimmesdale, speak "the very" emotional "truth" expressed by these writings, but by applying it to interpret Dickinson's biography, transform it "into the veriest falsehood" (*The Scarlet Letter,* "The Interior of a Heart," Chapter XI). The selves revealed by her letters and poems, then, are Dickinson's literary identities or ways of being, informed, to be sure, by the emotions of the actual woman who lived and wrote in Amherst but not faithfully representing them or revealing her. If they script an autobiography, it is a portrait of the artist.

      What portrait of the artist appears in the "Master" letters? Like the responses evoked by Bonnie Hayes's "Love Letter," made popular by the performance of Bonnie Raitt, what kind of story emerges deciphering or interpreting these depends very much on the desires of the reader (see epigraphs for this chapter). The house of the song's first line is variously imagined in the minds of the audience, as is the beloved to whom the house belongs, as is the car in which the speaker sits, as are the songs the speaker hears from the crooners on the radio. In this song, the audience constructs the beloved, and the song's main subject is not a lover longed for but the passionate longing itself; thus the love object is not so much the possible lover but the passion presently enjoyed. Similarly, interpreting the "Master" letters, each reader scripts his or her own beloved object. Since most readers are heterosexual or expect heterosexual amorous discourse and since Dickinson uses the male pronoun or "Sir" as the addressee of two of these, most interpretations confirm conventional expectations. But Rebecca Patterson's extensive study of Dickinson's letters and poems led her to quite different conclusions regarding the gender of a mysterious beloved's identity and to speculation about the poet's passion for Kate Anthon and Sue. Besides the context of erotic letters to those two women, textual facts of the documents themselves throw the gender identity of the beloved into question as well as raise more questions about genre. Briefly and document by document, I will scrutinize each of the drafts, specifically as records of her writing process.

* MARTHA NELL SMITH, *ROWING IN EDEN: REREADING EMILY DICKINSON,* UNIVERSITY OF TEXAS PRESS, 1992, P.108

~

Everything begun with the need to understand. To understand myself and my practice through the words of others, proceeded and accompanied by my continued interest in autobiography and biography as fictional constructs. The longer I thought about what my fixation on biography might signify, this area of inquiry started to appear suggestive and complex. I had to find a way to embrace it.

Just like when talking to someone or to no one in particular, aloud, you clarify your thoughts and make an order in your head, while writing, the ideas and reflections gain structure. And letters are thus a form of conversation. E-mail creates a distance to the person you correspond with –

more so than letters or phone calls, not to mention face-to-face meetings. This distance triggers the imagination. As in my email correspondence, which forms the bulk of my thesis; in most cases, I have never met my recipients.

The first e-mail brought about the writing of another one, and so on, resulting in this collection of texts.

Nearly two months of my life (from October 29 to December 31, 2014) was dedicated to a correspondence that has become more than a personal journal. These conversations, records and exchange of notes on (auto)biography have become me, my mes. At the same time, this collection could be a mirror in which one can see one's own, refracted reflection. During the period of letter-writing, sometimes it felt like talking to a wall or to myself, where the other, the supposed second half of the conversation, became a pretext to continue my own thoughts.

From the outset, I decided to contact people, who in one way or the other, inspired me and have influenced my practice – in order to pry from them additional specific information. And I am grateful that they helped to shape my view and understanding on the subjects that lie at the core of my research.

Among them are (in alphabetical order): James Benning – independent filmmaker and artist, whose project *Two Cabins* reconstructs H. D. Thoreau's and Ted Kaczynski's iconic cabins; James Frey – American writer, author of the controversial memoir *A Milion Little Pieces*; Jacob Korczynski – independent curator, whose project and publication *I See/ La Camera: I*, researched feminist aesthetic in the practices of Lucy Lippard and Babette Mangolte; Chris Kraus – a Los

Angeles-based writer and filmmaker, author of the novel *I Love Dick*, which is not a memoir but performs as one; Momus (Nicholas Currie) – artist, blogger, songwriter, author of the imagination triggering *The Book of Japans*; Carl E. Rollyson – biographer, author of *A Higher Forms of Cannibalism? Adventures in the Art and Politics of Biography*; Max Saunders – literary critic, author of the *Self Impression: Life Writing, Autobiografiction, and the forms of Modern Literature*; Lytle Shaw – New York-based poet and writer, author of a book about the search for a Swiss photographer, *The Moiré Effect*; David Shields, American writer, author of the *Reality Hunger: A Manifesto*; Sam Stephenson – writer, since 1997 has been studying the life and work of photographer W. Eugene Smith; Galen Strawson – British philosopher, author of a paper *Against Narrativity*, in which he argues against the claim that we need explicit narratives to develop fully as a person; Krisztina Toth – engaged in handwriting analysis.

I also would like to thank the graphologist Mrs. Marijke van der Linden, who made me realize a lot of things about myself.

On the following pages are texts of incipient ideas and other beginnings. I don't even know if all the people mentioned really exist. The most real they seem to me, was when I found them in my inbox.

W.T.
December 2014

On Wed, Oct 29, 2014, at 7:10 PM <dshields> wrote:

Hi, pls see my new book How litera-ture saved my life, which explores these questions quite directly. Ds

On Wed, Oct 29, 2014, at 8:35 PM <carollyson> wrote:

I can respond to some specific questions. I'm pleased to know you have found value in my work.

*

On Thu, Oct 30, 2014, at 00:08 AM <max.saunders> wrote:

Dear Weronika,
Many thanks for your kind words about my book. Your project sounds fascinating and in principle I'd be glad

to cooperate as long as it doesn't involve too much time -- I'm horribly busy at the moment! But by all means let me know more about what your practice involves, and how I might help.

all best,
Max

Dear Max,

Thank you so much for quick reply. I fully understand that you are very busy but it would be very important to me if you could give me any kind of reflections, notes on the matter of auto/biography as fictional constructs.

It could be short thought, anything that comes to your head and in your opinion might be worthy attention. The project is in a form of a letters and each of them gives me a point of references to continue and/or expand my point of view. Therefore any comment would be much appreciated.
Looking forward,

Very best,
Weronika.

On Fri, Oct 31, 2014, at 3:18 PM <weronikatrojanska> wrote:

Dear Carl,
Please find below some questions. I hope they are more or less clear... They

relate to the matter of biography itself as well as to my practice.

I also want to refer to my recent project (that I mentioned before) based on an endeavor to get closer to the person by analyzing and learning her handwriting. Having an access to Margot Zanstra's (ballerina and sculptress) personal archive, at her home and studio in Amsterdam, I started to work with the material I found there. As a result, the work consist also of a text that is a "mental documentation" of the process of learning Zanstra's handwriting, a peculiar dialog between me and her – the character that was my vision on Margot's figure.

> <

- How fixed could be fiction in biography?

- Who is the person – the protagonist of biography when she or he becomes fictionalized (in literature?) Can we talk at this moment as well of a fictional character?

- Who is the person that appears „between" the biographer and the protagonist of the biography?

- Does the person the biographer writes about inhabit in some measure his/her (the biographer) Self?

- When did you feel the closest to the person about whom you were writing? How did you know/noticed that?

- Could the biography be understood and manifested in a perfomative way (also as a learning process)?

- Do you think it is possible to understand/get to know the biography of someone else by adapting/reenacting particular facts/episodes from his or hers life? (e.g. learning the other person's handwriting, going to the places that she or he used to go etc.)

\- Do you think that this might be a way of preservation? Or/and translation?

\- Could it be seen as a way of becoming someone else?

\- Do you think that we carry inside us polyphonic (collective) biography? Consisting of all the lives that inspire/influence us?

\- Who is 'Margot Zanstra' then (in connection to the project)?

><

I hope is not too much I am asking for...

Thank you,
Weronika

On Fri, Oct 31, 2014, at 5:38 PM <carollyson> wrote:

It will take me some time to sort through the questions. And in some cases, I may ask for clarification. I will probably not answer the questions all at once, but one at a time, most likely.

*

On Sat, Nov 1, 2014, at 1:19 PM <carollyson> wrote:

How fixed is/could be fiction in biography?

I don't understand the question.

When the person that is the protagonist

<u>of the biography becomes fictionalize</u> <u>(in literature), who is she or he then?</u> <u>Can we talk at this moment as well of a</u> <u>fictional character?</u>

I deal with this issue in a section of my book, READING BIOGRAPHY, where I suggest a novel like Joyce Carol Oates's BLONDE can make Marilyn's mother a fictional character, and yet the way that character is presented, can make us think more deeply about the real person who was Marilyn's mother. Oates does a wonderful job of showing how from the child's (Marilyn's) point of view, her mother was terrifying because her behavior was so erratic, and children require parents to be stable and consistent.

*

<u>When did you feel the closest to the person about whom you were writing? How did you know/notice that?</u>
     Not sure about the second part of the question. The first part: I feel closest when I'm actually writing about the person, when I am thinking about how a certain event, a letter, or something someone said, fits into what I'm putting on the page at that moment. In other words, when I'm actually writing the story of a life, making it a narrative, I feel the closest to my subject. Anything else--say just talking about my subject is a poor substitute for the narrative I've written.

*

Do you think it is possible to under-
stand/get to know the biography of someone else by adapting/reenacting particular facts/episodes from his or hers
life? (e.g. learning the other person's
handwriting, going to the places that
she or he used to go etc.)

Some biographers make a real fetish of
going to the places where their subjects
lived or traveled. One of Graham Greene's biographers boasted about going
everywhere Greene went. Robert Caro
spent a lot of time in Texas where
Lyndon Johnson grew up, and so on.
I've done some of that, and occasionally
actually being in a place where my subject lived turned out to be important.
I could see how moving from Lynn
to Swampscott, Massachusetts, much

closer to the sea, opened up the world to Walter Brennan, whose biography I've just completed. But I don't think going to places associated with a biographical subject is necessarily necessary. Saul Bellow set a novel in Africa without going there. So why can't a biographer do the same thing? Both biographies and novels are works of the imagination. I don't think reading Rebecca West's handwriting gave me any insight into her character but it did make me feel closer to her because I was reading something she put in her own hand. That is an intangible reward but a valuable one to me.

On Mon, Nov 3, 2014, at 5:48 PM <gstrawson> wrote:

Dear Weronika

Thanks for this. This paper repeats some of the things I've said before, but may be useful.

Best wishes

Galen

Dear Galen,

Thank you for the quick reply and the paper *The Unstoried Life*, it will certainly be of use.

As I mentioned earlier I share the interest in what you called in *Against Narrativity*: the episodic self-experience, which somehow led me to understand the biography as compilation of fragments rather than narrative story. I have in mind what Nicholson Baker wrote in

U and I (by the way with reference to John Updike who you also mentioned) that „I remember almost nothing of what I read. What once was *Portrait of a Lady* is now for me only a plaid lap-blanket bobbing on the waves; *Anna Karenina* survives somehow as a picnic basket containing a single jar of honey". I feel much related to this.

In *Unstoried Life* you write: „I don't think an <<autobiographical narrative>> plays any significant role in how I experience the world, although I know that my present overall outlook and behavior is deeply conditioned by my genetic inheritance [...] I am creature who <<consider itself as itself, the same thinking thing in different times and places>>." I also don't think I can in any way relate myself to the narrative, seeing myself rooted in narration. Of course, as you mentioned afterwards, there is always a past, but we also cannot rely on memory. Sometimes even looking at myself in pictures taken a few months ago I cannot see the same person. I cannot relate to my feelings and memories, as they belong to someone else, but in a sense of a character in a movie or novel that you identify with in some way. I went yesterday to the Tim Etchells performance. I never met him in person before but we have been in touch through e-mail. I thought it would be nice to say „hello", so I approached him after the show, just to introduce myself, to give a real picture of the virtual. It was a very short, two-minute chitchat but after I had a feeling that we are both not who we thought we are. Nothing like disappointment, just as though the real body did not fit to the virtual soul... Like while writing we were other people... As while writing I was someone else. As I was writing someone else. And when I came back home I felt like this introduction didn't happen, as though I only imagined it in a daydream or saw someone enacting it... or read it in a newspaper.

In your paper you are quoting Erik Erikson: „various selves…make up a composite Self. These are constant and often shock like transitions between the selves... It takes indeed a healthy personality for the ‚I' to be able to speak out of all these conditions in such a way that at any moment it can testify to a reasonable coherent self". I totally agree with the idea of, as I like to call it - polyphonic Self. But what if the end the compilation of selves is not coherent and the form it will take depends on a given moment and it's unpredictable?

Very best,
Weronika.

P.S. I am not sure if I made myself clear, but also a part of my graduation project are texts or comments on/analysis of my practice done by other people from different fields. Therefore I want to ask you if you would be interested in helping me, in participating? It would be very important to me. However, I'd totally understand if you don't have time.

*

I'm not sure I can answer any more questions as you have set them out. But if you want to rephrase any of them, give it a try.

Dear Carl,
Right, the question might have been unclear, especially because it mostly refers to my practice in particular. (And probably my problems with English don't help either.)
What about these:
- Does writing biography (biographies) help you understand yourself?
- If (In what way) the protagonist of

biography differs from the character of a novel? If both might be based on existing persons, can we talk, in both cases, about the fictional characters?

- Do you think that writing biography is a way to maintain the life of memories about the other person?

- How would you define a „biography"?

Very best,
W.

On Tue, Nov 4, 2014, at 8:32 PM <weronikatrojanska> wrote:

I could see how moving from Lynn to Swampscott, Massachusetts, much closer to the sea, opened up the world to Walter Brennan, whose biography I've just completed.

Could you maybe explain to me in which way it opened up the world to Walther Brennan?

*

On Wed, Nov 5, 2014 at 2:44 PM <carollyson> wrote:

Lynn was a small town dominated by industries such as shoemaking. Swampscott with its coastal businesses dealt with a larger world, and Walter Brennan spent much time on the Swampscott docks observing people from all over the world.

On Wed, Nov 5, 2014 at 2:50 PM <carollyson> wrote:

Does writing biography (biographies) help you understand yourself?

Paul Murray Kendall in *The Art of Biography* states that every biography is also an autobiography. Certainly in my case, I have understood certain aspects of my own life by writing about the lives of others. My first ambition was to be an actor, and so I've been drawn to subjects like Marilyn Monroe, Dana Andrews, and Walter Brennan-- all of whom were willing to face adversity and persevere even when their careers seemed to be going anywhere. I was not willing to take the kinds of risks they did and so did not pursue an acting career after my initial attraction to it. And yet my desire to persevere-- no matter what -- even when certain subjects like Martha Gellhorn and Susan Sontag tried to stop me from writing about them is a quality I share with many of my subjects. And I consider the writing of biography a kind of performance. To be a biographer means trying to get inside another person in much the same way as an actor attempts to inhabit a character other than his own. And like an actor, I also draw on aspects of myself that I think I share with my subject.

On Wed, Nov 5, 2014, at 2:07 PM <weronikatrojanska> wrote:

Fantastic!

On Wed, Nov 5, 2014, at 9:22 PM <carollyson> wrote:

Good.

*

<u>How would you define „biography"?</u>

My story of a life. To me it's that simple, and also that complicated. It means my subject has an intrinsic. It means I don't say, as I have heard some biographers say, that I include only what illuminates the subject's work. It means I don't exclude sexual affairs even if they do not supposedly tell you anything about the subject's work. It means I leave out details (if they are not crucial) that inhibit the telling of my story. And it is MY story. Someone else's biography of the same subject will differ from mine. The answer to one biography is always another biography. I was amazed with a few responses on Goodreads that said there was nothing new in my Sylvia Plath biography. Such readers do not know how to read

*38

biography. All they had to do was set my Plath biography beside any other Plath biography and they would see the differences on virtually every page.

On Thu, Nov 6, 2014, at 7:57 PM <weronikatrojanska> wrote:

Can we say then that there is as many biographies as biographers? Or as many lives as points of view?

The comment on Sylvia Plath made me think of the readers of the biographies... Who does actually read biographies, and why? Personally, I've never been very interested in narrative. My mind is pretty selective, I guess, and remembers only episodes and parts that really struck me while reading; so somehow I found all kinds of chronological, historical, thousand-pages biographies pretty boring... but I can understand, for example also in connection to the last question I asked you, the attempt to try to understand myself through reading about someone else's life, or maybe more, looking for clues as to how to change my own life...

On Thu, Nov 6, 2014, at 7:58 PM <carollyson> wrote:

The answer to your question is yes.

On Thu, Nov 6, 2014, at 8:52 PM <weronikatrojanska> wrote:

What do you think, which other ‚tricks’/ ’strategies’ can a biographer use to get closer to the person? (This question is particularly important for my practice as an artist :)

*

On Fri, Nov 7, 2014, at 1:02 PM <carollyson> wrote:

Talking to anyone who knew my subject no matter how many times others may have interviewed the same person.

On Fri, Nov 7, 2014 at 1:07 PM <carollyson> wrote:

<u>If (In what way) the protagonist of biography differs from the character of a novel? If both might be based on existing persons, can we talk, in both cases, about the fictional characters?</u>
  All characters on the page are

constructs, the product of language. But characters in biography have to be assessed against other biographies and other evidence.

Dear Weronika,

Thanks for your interest in *The Moiré Effect*. Was this something you read in a class? Or did you come across it on your own?

I like thinking about biography as a limit condition; not an essence -- so your projects sounds interesting. The best way for me to be involved is for you to just invite me to give a lecture or do a mini-seminar at your university; depending on how the visit is structured, I could do critiques as part of it. I would welcome the excuse to go to Holland, since I have an ongoing project on Dutch art.

Best,
Lytle Shaw

On Fri, Nov 7, 2014, at 6:15 PM <weronikatrojanska> wrote:

Dear Lytle Shaw,
Thank you so much for the reply and suggestions. To be honest, I haven't been taking into account such options, as the thing I am working on now is based primarily on e-mail exchange; but let me think about it!
And about *The Moiré Effect* – it was actually recommended to me at Motto in Berlin, while I was still engaged in my project on fictional artist.

Very best,
Weronika

*

On Sat, Nov 8, 2014, at 10:54 PM <momasu> wrote:

Hello Weronika,

Thanks for writing. It's an interesting topic, though of course there are lots of clichés to avoid if possible.

For some reason I remembered something the humanist psychologist Liam Hudson wrote in his book (from the 1960s) *Contrary Imaginations*. He was doing psychometric research on schoolboys, and grouped them into „convergers" and „divergers". These are different thinking styles, which line up roughly with the division between the sciences and the humanities. Convergers want to narrow things down to „the one right answer" whereas divergers like to throw up a plethora of entertaining possibilities, connecting things playfully, ambiguously and inconclusively.

The part that interests me is that although you'd think the divergers were more revealing of their selves, more extravert, in fact Hudson says this isn't so. Both types of boy (he only studied boys) are controlling what the world learns about them. Hudson calls this „rival systems of defense". You can either hide by being taciturn and introverted (like a scientist) or hide behind a multiplicity of entertaining masks (like an actor or an artist or a trickster). In fact, because the show-off artist-actor-trickster-type doesn't seem to be hiding anything, he's in fact hiding it more effectively. Instead of answering „That's private!" he'll put on a funny voice, use sarcasm, make a joke, tell you something then tell you it was a lie, quote someone else, tell the truth as if it were a lie, give six contradictory answers, and so on.

Something else I map this to is Ernst Kretschmer's division of schizoids into „anaesthetic" and „hyperaesthetic" types. I guess this is from his 1925 book *Physique and Character*. It starts with his description of the hyperaesthetic:

"Timid, shy, with fine feelings, sensitive, nervous, excitable…
Abnormally tender, constantly wounded… <<all

nerves.>> …

[Hyperaesthetics] feel all the harch, strong colo-
urs and tones of everyday life… as shrill, ugly…
even to the extent of being physically painful.
Their autism is a painful cramping of the sell into
itself. They seek as far as possible to avoid and de-
aden all stimulation from the outside. (1925, pp.
155-161)

Descriptively, and in contrast to hypera-
esthetic/avoidant, Kretschmer portrayed the ana-
esthetic/schizoid personality as follows:

We feel that we are in contact with something flavourless, boring… What is there in
the deep under all these masks? Perhaps there is
nothing, a dark, hollow-eyed nothing – affecti-
ve anaemia. Behind an ever-silent façade, which
twitches uncertainly with every expiring whim –
nothing but broken pieces, black rubbish heaps,
yawning emotional emptiness, or the cold breath
of an arctic soullessness. (1925, p. 150)."

This book seems to have had an influence on the poet Robert Lowell, who explained his avoidance of military service by the fact that he was the first type: that his sensitivity would make active service unbearable for him! He also described his first wife as „all air and nerve" in the poem *Man and Wife,* which seems to be a reference to Kretschmer's description of the hyperaesthetic.

Anyway, this is just me gossiping. I don't know how helpful it is to you. This sort of personality theory is deeply unfashionable, but I love it. „The cold breath of an arctic soullessness"!

Nick

*

On Sun, Nov 9, 2014, at 2:34 PM <weronikatrojanska> wrote:

Dear Carl,

I really like the thought that the chracters on the page are products of language; even when we talk about the other person we always „put him/her into words".

But could you maybe give example(s) of what you mean by <u>other evidence</u>?

Thank you!

On Sun, Nov 9, 2014, at 3:36 PM <carollyson> wrote:

Other evidence: court records, birth certificates, immigration records, military service, etc. memoirs, photographs, films, diaries, letters, receipts, bills or checks.

*

On Mon, Nov 10, 2014, at 9:31 PM <weronikatrojanska> wrote:

Dear Nick,

Thank you for such a quick and comprehensive reply.

Your notes sound very interesting to me. I've never been delving much into details of psychoanalysis; although it sounds important and obvious, but I somehow never had the patience to dig deeper than schizophrenia and personality disorders. If so, I went more into the direction of neuroscience, looking for answers in theories of ‚split-brain’, ‚multiple self’, ‚fictional self’ etc.

It used to be in fashion to be a ‚schizophrenic’ artist/writer though. To some extent, I grew up in a messed up atmosphere of the Polish avant-garde Gombrowicz, Schultz, and Witkacy (the latter even called his cat "Schizofrenia";) Actually, I never thought about it before...

Liam Hudson was involved in ‚making art’ himself. It’s interesting that for him that the psychological typecasting had been a matter of cultural choice rather than innate tendency. In *The Maltese Falcon* Hammett made a digression telling a story of a man named Flitcraft. One day he left his home and never returned home, with a desire to change his life and become another person; but in the end he eventually found himself creating the same situations, from which he tried to escape. One can always try to be someone else, whether disappearing and abandoning current life or taking on the identity of someone else. But how do you know who you have been and whether the person you are becoming is not just yourself? What if it is the other way around? What if there are more personalities that you should adopt to become yourself? Or maybe being yourself is impossible then?

I think I don't have much faith in doubles. There is always a risk of jumping from one thing to the other, with a need of designations. I want to believe that personality is a learning process, a sketch of various possibilities open to us.

Similar with identity - it's an ongoing project that includes constructing a biography. How, and if, one can change an identity partially?

I am trying with my mind and/or body to write a biography of someone else. With each person something always stays with me (whether his or her handwriting or the time they used to wake up), how the "I" can be a „storage" for episodes of biographies of others. And therefore my Self becomes a polyphonic (collective) biography.

So yes... hide behind a multiplicity of entertaining masks (like an actor or an artist or a trickster). In fact, because the show-off artist-actor-trickster-type doesn't seem to be hiding anything, he's in fact hiding it more effectively.

I would be very happy if this conversa-

tion would continue...
Very best,
W.

*

Dear Carl,

Thank you so much for all replies. I could almost rephrase your words to talk about myself, my practice. You say that your first ambition was to be an actor, and so you've been drawn to subjects like Marylyn Monroe, Dana Andrews, and Walter Brennan. "I was not willing to take the kinds of risk they did and so did not pursue an acting career after my initial attraction to it". Sometimes I wonder if my whole in-terest in biographies, lives of others put into words (or into language, as you wrote to me in the other letter that the characters are „the product of language") is not drawn by my inner desire to be a writer. I just realized that my attraction also somewhat concentrates around figures like Kathy Acker, Robert Lowell, Susan Sontag, Chris Kraus. The lives they lead and the (their) lives put on paper. Lucy Lippard wrote in *I see/You Mean* that she lives two lives simultaneously. "This one written here and my English one".

It also appears very quaint to me to notice that my interest has been turning into female figures, as I was always saying that I am not very fond of feminine writing (if it's proper to put it that way).

I had this impression that it does not speak to me. Maybe it has something to do with what Babette Mangolte said about our bisexuality - not in a meaning of sexual attraction but rather having in mind that we are both male and female at the same time. Two personalities inhabit you - male and female, but in fact, there is no distinction between them. So we live them both at once. And maybe then the male part of my identity was more dominant. And now, the contrary, or maybe it has become more balanced.

I also feel especially related to your description of a ‚biography as a kind of performance'. „To be a biographer means trying to get inside another person in much the same way as an actor attempts to inhabit a character other than his own". It's funny, just yesterday I told my friend that I try to avoid acting (as he also referred to drama, acting, theater), but I am still fascinated by the idea of impersonation.

In a sense, our personalities are collection of others, people that we met, admired, wanted to be, dreamed of, desired or slept with. Even when I am writing this now I create a character that would become familiar to you, but how do you know that it is me, that it is not totally invented?

My Very Best,
Weronika

P.S. I guess we went through all I asked already... Thank you so much again! It's very helpful to me.

On Thu, Nov 13, 2014, at 3:21 PM <carollyson> wrote:

Ok. Keep me posted about your work.

By the way, I'm writing an article about the place of biography in academia for a volume titled THE BIOGRAPHI-CAL TURN, edited by Hans Renders.

On Thu, Nov 13, 2014, at 3:36 PM <jamesfrey> wrote:

Happy to help, answer questions, whatever you need. I'm in Amsterdam right now if you want to meet in-person.

On Thu, Nov 13, 2014, at 3:46 PM <james_frey> wrote:

Or we can do email, or use facebook.

On Thu, Nov 13, 2014, at 4:38 PM <weronikatrojanska> wrote:

Thank you for such a quick reply. The project based primarily on e-mail exchange, but it would be great to meet in person! How long are you staying in Amsterdam? It's such a coincidence, the only contact I could find was facebook, and then I saw the picture from Amsterdam. Nice.

On Thu, Nov 13, 2014, at 6:29 PM <james_frey> wrote:

I'm here until Saturday morning. About to head out for dinner, but back around 8:30 or free tomorrow before 1:00.

On Thu, Nov 13, 2014, at 4:38 PM <weronikatrojanska> wrote:

Tomorrow would be better for me. I also have time until around 1pm. Just let me know where and when. Looking forward!

On Thu, Nov 13, 2014, at 7:16 PM <james_frey> wrote:

I'll send you a note when I get up. Only thing I want to do is go to the Rijksmuseum.

On Thu, Nov 13, 2014, at 8:06 PM <weronikatrojanska> wrote:

OK. We can maybe meet somewhere around the Rijks? I have a studio visit at 1pm so I need to be back by then. Best. W.

*

On Fri, Nov 14, 2014, at 10:43 AM <james_frey> wrote:

Finishing up an interview.
Heading over soon

On Fri, Nov 14, 2014, at 10:52 AM <weronikatrojanska> wrote:

I need around half an hour to get there, and don't have internet on my phone...

On Fri, Nov 14, 2014, at 10:54 AM <james_frey> wrote:

Can you text?

On Fri, Nov 14, 2014, at 10:56 AM <weronikatrojanska>

wrote:

Yes.
Around Rijksmuseum would be good?

On Fri, Nov 14, 2014, at 10:57 AM <james_frey> wrote:

Yeah

On Fri, Nov 14, 2014, at 11:00 AM <weronikatrojanska> wrote:

What time more or less?

On Fri, Nov 14, 2014, at 11:03 AM <james_frey> wrote:

11:30?
Any interest in going into the museum?

I have to be back at 1:00

On Fri, Nov 14, 2014, at 11:04 AM <weronikatrojanska> wrote:

Let's say 11:40? I'm leaving now.

On Fri, Nov 14, 2014, at 11:07 AM <james_frey> wrote:

Cool
In front of museum?

*

On Sun, Nov 16, 2014, at 12:00 PM <weronikatrojanska> wrote:

Hi James; was nice to meet you and I hope you enjoyed Amsterdam. It would

be great if you can write me your e-mail
address. Thanks! W

*

On Mon, Nov 17, 2014, at 4:09 PM <jgbenning> wrote:

yes, it looks interesting, but this sentence wasn't clear to me:
„I want to ask people from different
fields (from graphologist, psychiatrist
to theater director) to say something/
comment/criticize my practice, also in
a relation to the question how could be
possible to become someone else."

On Mon, Nov 17, 2014, at 6:52 PM <ckraus> wrote:

hi Weronika,
Thanks for your note, and appreciation.

The questions you raise sound really interesting, and close to something I'm working on now-a critical biography of the American writer Kathy Acker. I'll be in London in January to talk about biography/autobiography, friction, proximity, etc., at an event called „Plastic Words" hosted by Ravens Row.

I'm sorry I can't be more helpful -- have many commitments, and it would take time and thought to really engage with what you are doing. But I wish you the best with your work.
thanks and all best,
Chris

On Mon, Nov 17, 2014, at 8:20 PM <weronikatrojanska> wrote:

Dear James,

Thank you for the reply.

„I want to ask people from diffcrent fields (from graphologist, psychiatrist to theater director) to say something/ comment/criticize my practice, also in a relation to the question how could be possible to become someone else."

This applies to the project in general and refers to my other works I did. I invited people not only connected to art world to say something on the subject of auto/biography as a fictional construct(s). Basically, I am interested in a format of conversation, the form of which depends largely on the individual person. Any kind of reflections, feedback, notes would be appreciated. Looking forward to hearing from you, Very best,

On Mon, Nov 17, 2014 at 8:30 PM < jgbenning>wrote:

yes, but i need to know what you mean by this: subject of auto/biography as a fictional construct(s).

On Mon, Nov 17, 2014, at 9:46 PM <weronikatrojanska> wrote:

Working for a quite long time on a project(s) involving fictional (nonexisting) artists, my interest turned into biography itself. If we are able to invent life of someone else and easily make it real (by making people believe in him or her), probably we are doing the same on a daily basis, inventing (glossing over the facts, mixing fake memories with real ones, etc.). We are always caught up in a complex net of negotiations with our own past experiences; reconfiguring elements that in turn become a story that is consider to be the truth. How we associate with one memory (of a person, event, feeling, piece of mu-sic, conversation, etc.) with another, is in-tricate and varied and is being used to 'compose our life' and the sense of the self.

On Mon, Nov 17, 2014, at 22:20 PM <weronikatrojanska> wrote:

Dear James,

It was very nice to meet you.

What I knew about you before was that you are undeniably one of the tabloid stars of literature, have a couple fan-pa-ges, and was more than once, hauled onto Oprah Winfrey's red carpet, who on her show, first sang your praises, only later to douse you with criticism and, eventually, apologize. "Go Away", "James Fray Hasn't Given Up on Writing", "Million Little Lies", screamed the headlines from the Daily Mail to Vanity Fair. Author most known for *A Million Little Pieces* - a book that has been accused of being nothing else than a fabricated memoir. It's not really my favorite kind of literature - when the main character talks about his rehab, describing details of how his teeth were pulled out without anesthesia. But I tried to get through it, especially when we were about to meet.

So, you came. You had an almost com-pletely shaved head, narrow face, small cunning eyes, were chewing gum, and had a fast, stiff gait, and an Ohioan accent. Jumping between one famous

Dutch painting to the other (you wanted to see just the old, masterpieces section) I tried to explain more or less what's going on in my practice, why and what I need you for, why I cannot get along well with the city, if I liked New York and... I didn't even pay attention to whether you were listening. And then we stopped at Rembrandt's "Nightwatch". I noticed that you cannot stay standing still for more than a minute. "What is this painting so famous for?" – you asked rolling your eyes in a funny way, shrugged and stealthily made a photo with your I-phone. I was wondering for a second if you were going to show "Rembrandt" to your kids. It doesn't matter how many you have, as the amount changes depending on a source I am reading. Approximately from one to three, I would say. We moved forward.

After flitting by a few other rooms we accidently ended up at the same spot. In the background of the painting, behind the helmeted figure, an eye and a beret that appear from the dark have been identified as Rembrandt himself. At least so says the description. We slowly started to walk towards the exit. – "Do you know Richard Prince?", you asked me. "He's a good friend of mine. I should put you in touch with him. He knows everything about what you are talking about. His whole biography is invented."

I'd have sent you an e-mail but you never gave me your address.
Nevertheless, I wish you all the best.
W.

*

Dear Weronika Trojanska,

Thank you for reaching out to me. Thank you for your kind words about my work.

Your project is interesting.
The first thing that comes to mind for me is the practice of drama, acting, theater, and also the practice of writing songs and lyrics in the voice of another person and then singing from that perspective. In both cases it's about inhabiting the other person, not so much analyzing or describing the other person, but being them. It can be done. But it can't be done if one is expected to stick to facts. Hence your mentioning fiction.

I'm not sure how I can help you directly. I'm very busy. But your project sounds terrific.

My best, and well wishes to you, and gratitude for reaching out to me.

Sam

*

On Thu, Nov 20, 2014, at 12:59 PM <weronikatrojanska> wrote:

Dear Chris,

Thank you for the reply.

Actually, recently, when I was doing my research on Elizabeth Hartwick and Robert Lowell, I stumbled across your article in „The Believer" on Kathy Acker. I found it especially interesting also in relation to my current work, which is primarily based on e-mail conversations. I haven't been reading much of Acker's but the way she approached her persona is very inspiring to me. All characters seem to speak the same voice, as they are a monologue of the same person. I really like this polyphony. In my practice the gestures and episodes of the lives of others are the voices and what I'm trying somehow to investigate is then whether my Self could become the ‚collective biography'? I like to call it ‚appropriations', which I found very relevant then to Acker's „plagiarization" of other selves (literary sources). I remember that I read somewhere the interview where she was asked if, dragging herself into the singular „I" would

be the death of Kathy Acker as a writer',
and she simply replied „Yeah, it sure is".

Anyway, those are just my personal di-
gressions.
I hope I will be able to come to London
in January, it sounds fascinating.

All my best,
Weronika

On Thu, Nov 20, 2014, at 7:03 PM <weronikatrojanska> wrote:

Dear Sam,

Thank you so much for the reply and
nice words.

It's really interesting that you mention
writing and performing lyrics and songs
- it somehow broadens my perspective.

In my practice, I am trying to avoid acting itself. Firstly, because it mostly involves the character assigned to particular role in a specific situation, time and space and allow being one character at time, when I am more interested in possible polyphonies. Secondly, because of the associations of the art world with this particular scene and all people committed to this world – like actors. "… The knowledge that we need to be true to ourselves, but that the best way to be truthful is through the use of somewhat artificial means forces all of us to an extent, to be actors in the art world" (as wrote P. Helguera). But of course it is still a lot about inhabiting. I think it might resemble more the process when an actor is preparing for a new role – learning the attitudes and traits of the character; as well as the idea that all the previous roles/personas still reside in the performer. It also reminds me of Antonin Artaud, who suggested that inhabiting a double may result in being more real. It does not tolerate its limitations. I like to think about the biography as a double or a shadow that follows you–that is susceptible to manipulations, but will never be able to represent yourself (be your representation). And I read recently in a text by Lesilie Scalapino on Kathy Acker that "autobiography is fiction: the same one is consuming (or being) itself".

All my best,
Weronika

*

On Sun, Dec 7, 2014 at 5:52 PM <jacob.korczynski> wrote:

Dear Weronika,

Thank you for your message. I'm glad you enjoyed the presentation I made with Babette in Amsterdam last week, and my research into her film *The Ca-mera: Je, La Camera: I* and Lucy Lippard's novel *I See/You Mean*. Besides the book that documents my research published by If I Can't Dance, the best reference I can share regarding the tension between autobiography and self--portraiture is a text by the Canadian artist Steve Reinke where he is writing about the work of another Canadian artist, Deirdre Logue:
http://deirdrelogue.com/writing/against_autobiography.html

I hope it is helpful. I wish you all the best with your research and thesis project.
Jacob

*

On Wed, Dec 10, 2014, at 6:44 PM <weronikatrojanska> wrote:

Dear Jacob,

Thank you so much for the reply.

What I found particularly interesting and worthy of attention in your research *I See/La Camera: I* is the connection between the language and photographic images and hence – the self-portraiture. I am not "very visual" in my artistic practice, thus mostly my source of references is drawn from literature, neuroscience etc. So the perspective of encountering the problem of the self as withdrawn from self-portraiture (images) is definitely something that might broaden my point of view. Regarding the psychologist Michael Gazzaniga, the Self is a fiction created by our brain, I've been posing myself a question – what is the self-portrait then?

You wrote that "Language and photography are laid out awaiting formation and cohesion, connected not by casual narrative but a series of spaces", which also relates very much to my interest in "episodic self-experience": one does not figure oneself, considered as a self, as something that was there in the past and will be there in the future.

In some ways it refers also to the text of Steve Reinke you sent me. In *Against Autobiography* he wrote that "In writing, self-portrait is often referred to as a sketch, and tends to be more descriptive than narrative and one can have but one authentic autobiography but an endless number of self-portraits."

There are some issues on autobiography that he raises, which are a little problematic for me and I need to think through before I say that I don't agree with them. Reinke assumes the point of view on autobiography from the perspective of written history or account of life: "Typically, the autobiography is a prose" – he says. Taking into account the dictionary definition – I won't argue much here. But then he speaks of "the act of autobiography [as] not active, performative, but reflective. Autobiography requires an act of removal. The subject must step out of the narrative stream of life events and recount, remember, reflect from a position that is inactive, neutral, removed. And moreover, autobiography has the goal of arriving, through its backward journey […]". But isn't the act of arriving backward just the performative aspect?

Reshaping life by recollections, conscious and unconscious omissions and distortions. As you said, the authority of autobiography is abstained through the fluidity of fiction. The narration of life is unsettled by constant editing of our story (stories). For Reinke there remains a dream of autobiography that consists entirely of an account of its own writing, or let's try to imagine an autobiography as automatic writing. I would leave the retrospective function more for the memoir then. I read recently in an old issue of "Bookforum" that when Chris Kraus published *Aliens* she didn't consider it as a memoir, because memoir, she writes is, "in the right now" of the present tense. 'Her characters fire off love letters, read books, complain about still unfinished work, feel shame. A memoir would bring closure to life, but she tells it now, while living, with the author being a "channel" for the culture: "It's passing through my body".

Thanks a lot,
Very best
Weronika.

*

On Sun, Dec 28, 2014, at 7:52 PM <tothkri>wrote:

Dear Weronika,

Sorry for my late reply. I had a busy week with my family in NL during the Christmas time and before that I was busy with the preparation. I hope my reply is not late!

Hope you had a nice Christmas!

Your graduation thesis is very interesting! I will reply you in couple of days, then I take my silence period to think it over and write down my sentences for you.

Where are you from?
Why did you choose this unique topic? (who, what inspired you?)

I'm wondering what kind of other people have you interviewed before. You ask people with specific professions for your thesis or..?

What is the deadline for your thesis? What are your plans for 2015 after graduation?

Wish you good luck! Success! :)
I'll come back to you in 2 days with my answer.

Kind regards,
Krisztina Toth

*

Dear Krisztina,

Thank you so much for your message, it's just in time :) and I hope you had a great holiday as well.

I came from Poland and as I wrote previously and I live currently in Amsterdam. I think my interest in auto/biography started somehow with the project about the fictional artist that I had been working on some years ago. Somewhere there as well also bustled about the handwriting, as I had to invent the manual records of his writings.

For the purposes of my thesis I have contacted people that might influence my practice and who have an understanding of the subject of my interest: a biographer, a writer, a philosopher, artists/filmmakers, a songwriter and an art coach, among others. I have to deliver the paper by the middle of

January (the defense is at the end of the month) and in June we have a practical diploma.

All the best and looking forward to reading your thoughts!

Weronika

*

On Wed, Dec 31, 2014, at 00:04 AM <tothkri> wrote:

Hi Weronika,
Many thanks for your answers!

Let me write some info about me: I'm from Budapest, Hungary. I live in Eindhoven, NL since 2010. I'm 34 years old.

I ran into graphology in 2004 at my college's job fair. I went for a quick (10 minutes) analysis to get some help for job interviews. What are my strengths and weaknesses. I wrote a 1 page letter and I was so amazed when a graphologist completely described me! I recognized myself! We never met before, so she didn't know about me anything!

This was a main point in my life, when I decided, when I start to work, I will study graphology.

Now this is my passion and I would like to use this method in helping young people to find their right studies and jobs.

In Amsterdam for sure you can find many artists, filmmakers. Best place to stay! :)

Marijke is a professional graphologist. She has much more work experience than me. I just finished my graphologist studies in 2010.

I'm sorry in advance if I write similar/ same things than Marijke already told you.

I would like to start with doodles. Doodles are randomly lines, curves, independent from any languages.

Sometimes we do it during a phone call or during a lesson at school.

Would you like to play with me? :-)
Take a paper and a pen and imagine the following feelings: angriness, madness, stressed, anxious, go crazy.
Then please make some doodles…
What did you draw? :-)

Okay, now please think about harmony, good/positive feelings, happiness, „I'm fine" feelings. Now draw some doodles. What did you draw?

If you read further you can read the answer.

Instinctively everybody draws the follow-
-ing:
1. doodle with feelings of anger, stress:
barbed lines with big pressure, strong edges
like a crocodile tooth
2. doodle with feelings of happiness, harmony: fully curved lines, continuously
drawn and the pressure is normal or lighter
than the 1st doodle

Did you draw the same?? :-)

Interesting, isn't it?

Handwriting analysis is based on experiences. Many great researchers in the past
spend their whole life collecting letters
and asking the owner to describe him/

herself.

So the researchers created groups like who speaks a lot, who is extrovert... etc... and they try to find common signs in the handwritings. It was a load of a job and much administration. You can imagine, when now we can read out more than 100 features from the handwriting.

I must write down some names: Max Pulver, Ludwig Klages, Jean-Hippolyte Michon, Aristoteles, Goethe (!)
If you google these names, you can find much information about them.

Like many PhD students they worked hard. :) They wrote many books about graphology.

It definitely works and I am still shocked when I describe someone from his/her handwriting and he/she gives feedback, that I'm right! :-)

Going back to movements.

This year I've been to a workshop. We did some games. One was that when we worked in couples. We needed to take an empty A4 size paper and 1-1 pen. Then the exercise was to move the pens on the paper. Both of us. It was not said to draw something object!

I was with a man (around 30 years old) and actually we started to „dance" on the paper! I really enjoyed it! I had a feeling like we were ice skating on the paper, the pen is the skate, the hand is our body. :) I felt good harmony with the pen-mate. :-)

We moved here, there, we draw many, many curves and we moved the pen smoothly. None of us wanted to draw anything specific, just we enjoyed the time on the paper. We never bumped… and none of us draw any edges…just curves!

We did it for like 2-3 mins.

Other couples draw something specific together: flower, house, nice beach view. Only our paper was full of curves, un-specified, randomly lines.

Unfortunately nowadays we write less and less. Even in the US some of the states they stopped teaching hand-writing! I think it is a huge mistake, because via the handwriting our psy-chomotoric skills are improving, it is good for studying and improving other skills for the future ages. It is a very important skill which is needed to be improved!

Might you have met many men who always told you that their handwriting is ugly and that they just don't like writing… or they choose to write with capitals.

I studied that unfortunately men have less soft motorical hands when they are 7 to have a successfully writing skills… that's why for them writing is more challenging, compared to girls. They have less success, so men don't like writing by hand.

Girls have most of the time legible, nice, wavy handwriting, due to their biological status of their hands are better improved at the age of 7.

Rafael Schermann: he was a great man who looked at handwriting as a symbol and figured out how the owner of the handwriting looks like.

Here are 2 interesting links:
http://dreamhawk.com/interesting-people/schermann-graphologist--extraordinary-superminds/
http://www.encyclopedia.com/doc/1G2-3403804008.html

Actually, I use symbolism during the analysis. It's fun, when I find a heart shape oval (this means that the person is in love or hungry for love)... or once a man had a signature which looked like a bike, and when I told him that I think you love cycling...and he was shocked and asked how I knew?

I explained to him where can I find the 2 wheels and other parts of the bike in his signature. He was amazed because he never saw this from his signature. Subconscious works! :)

Or...another example...a photographer has a signature in a frame (rectangle). :)

It is a nice game to check some signatures by art people and try to find out their profession or passion.
It is not always there and not always shows happy, positive signs...

Graphology is a complex science. I've studied psychology, biology, history of graphology, how to make good sentences in the analysis, how to measure the letters, margins... and study, then practice the signs and their meanings (hundreds!).
Like a doctor listens to the symptoms from the patient, then he knows which disease he has and knows also the solution for that. A graphologist can read out from the handwriting when a per-

son is an alcoholic/drug user/depressive/bipolar.

For now I think this is what I can write you. If I have more things to say, I will write it.
I hope it fulfills your inquiry.

If you have any questions, do not hesitate to write me! :)
Wish you good luck for the thesis and please let me know how it went!

I wish you a wonderful 2015!
Kind regards,
Krisztina Toth

On Wed, Dec 31, 2014, at 2:35 PM <weronikatrojanska> wrote:

Hi Krisztina,

Thanks again for your all-embracing answer. I will take a closer look in the next few days (as I am traveling tomorrow from Poland to Amsterdam) and I will get back to you if I have any queries. I was amazed myself at how exciting and fascinating graphology can be. My curiosity pushed me pretty pragmatically into its direction, into a curiosity about my handwriting, when I noticed that after learning Margot Zanstra's (Dutch sculptress who lived in Amsterdam) penmanship my own remains different and wanting to find out what this really means I finally contacted graphologists. That's how I met Marijke, as she was the one of those who responded and, as she admitted, was also curious whether I was not a bit crazy trying to be someone else… as she said: "I was a little bit afraid that you were too obsessed" ;) During our first meeting I got a little "scared" of how much she could say about me only based on my writing and not only about my personal traits but also the artistic ones: that I have a desire for beautiful things, feeling for colors and all that but I prefer concepts and ideas. This apparently has been reflected in the analysis of my handwriting samples before and after the copying/learning sessions: "You acted controlled, more than enough, so I see now less tension. I think it causes your artistic doings, because you can be much more interested in concept and ideas but you have also the unconscious – it's indeed a little therapy for you. It's abnormal when your handwriting doesn't change.

Through eventual experience, emotions, people, you have changes in habits etc. and then your handwriting evolves. I don't see that there is anything wrong. So, be happy!" ;)

Thank you and all the most beautiful in New Year!
Weronika

EPILOGUE

On Sat, Jan 10, 2015, at 9:23 PM <weronikatrojanska>
wrote:

*I, always with I…..one always starts
with I…….and ends with I.* [1]

I see on these pages a record of myself in
a particular moment, like a portrait photograph. A self-portrait made by someone else.
But also in the company of small effigies
of people with whom I talked to. And all
together it creates a group portrait of the
merger between myself and them – an
(auto)biography and its fictional constructs.

What has been generated during
this period of two months of writing letters
acts now as a critical reflection. This e-mail
exchange has become a possible model of
production. One of the possible scenarios.

1) B. S. JOHNSON, *TRAWL*, SECKER & WARBURG, 1966

AFTERWARDS

Through his dreamy land he could see himself, as if another life and like another person (...) it was if he must look around for someone else to share his joy with: for someone to whom he might tell the thing, for his own relief.

Walter Pater

Everything we hold becomes a tool. Even people. Even you.

Karel Capek

I am sitting on a bench next to myself.

Robert Ashley

Who I am now I won't be in the moment you read this. I don't feel comfortable with a concept that your life is like a story, a narrative of events and actions. I probably won't recognize myself in these letters by the time you have them, or maybe I already no longer identify with them.

While writing this, I am visiting my family home, surrounded by the people who know me since the day I was born, and by the things that I am most familiar with: photographs, books, stories – it all can bring me back to particular moments, persons, but not myself.

I don't think I have a strong linear sense of time. How can you believe in linearity if sometimes something that happened a few years ago seems as vivid as yesterday and at other times, your life can turn upside down in one day, or better – in an hour or a second. The autobiographical time bears within itself a wide range of connections, such as coincidence, choice, fate, chance, contingency and déjà-vu. „And these we may apply when we view our portrait photograph"[1]. In this context poet John Ashbery spoke out beautifully about seeing a movie of ourselves:

If you could see a movie of yourself you would realize that this is true. Movies show us our-selves as we had not yet learned to recognize us – something in the nature of daily being or happen-ing that quickly gets folded over into ancient history like yesterday's newspaper, but in so doing a new face has been revealed, a surface on which a new phrase may be written before it rejoins history, or it may remain blank and do so anyway. [2]

In her essay *On Beginning* Mary Ruffle wrote that from the day we learn our first word "we each only really speak one

1) J. BROCKMEIER, *AUTOBIOGRAPHICAL TIME*, IN: BAMBERG, MICHAEL AND ALLYSSA MCCABE, NARRATIVE IDENTITY. SPECIAL ISSUE OF "NARRATIVE INQUIRY" 10:1 (2000). 2000. 265 PP. (PP. 51–73)
2) J. ASHBERY, *THE SYSTEM*, IN: "THE PARIS REVIEW", NO. 53, WINTER 1972

sentence in our lifetime"[3]. Following this trail it could be said that we also write (in our minds) one lifelong letter to ourselves, trying to understand the mysteries of our personalities, daily existence, relations with others and so forth. "This letter's taken almost a year to write and therefore it's became a story" – wrote Chris Kraus in *I Love Dick*.

We think that by putting something on paper, giving it a structure or narrative will help to organize and understand our self (selves) or to have a control over it. In fact, identity is an ongoing process, a project that includes constructing a personal biography. But the biography is just one possible scenario, just one of the scripts that we wrote after we had followed it.

It's only the others who put the puzzles of your life into sequential pieces, giving it the narrative it becomes. And in the case of this paper, you – the reader – are

3) M. RUEFLE, *ON BEGINNING*, IN: MADNESS, RACK AND HONEY: COLLECTED LECTURES, WAVE BOOKS, 2012

the only witness of my self, in the period of wiring these letters. I became, for you, a fictional persona, indistinguishable from any other character appearing on these pages.

The characters here exist. In real life they are significant figures in the culural field, but not only. They are writers, scholars, filmmakers, philosophers, psychologists. All these people with whom I had contact eventually became the characters in the narrative of these letters, and moreover, the characters I created. The protagonists of my story. I must admit I was a little disappointed because in the e-mail exchanges, they often didn't meet my expectations and often didn't extend the conversations to make them an on-going discussion, not only a germ. The dream would be to create a correspondence that is something between the letters of Robert Lowell to Elizabeth Bishop and Kathy Acker to McKenzie Wark. But most of them were only like a one-off date or a short-lived romance that, for now, have never turned into anything more.

So it was because of them, of me with them, that I started to become fascinated with a variety of impersonations. Fictional avatars. In order to see in the mirrors of the others, in the others as mirrors, the contested and unfinished self as a site of multivalent subjectivities. How to build an autobiography (without writing one) using other people as triggers? And activate presence and absence (of the desired person) at the same time? The associated risk entails the matter of authorship, selfhood, representation and the division between fact and fiction. Is it not true that the most attractive and seductive is what appears to be a threat or a danger?

The biography acts as a double – a parallel system (idea, environment) in which the assumptions of our life remain but are interpreted in ways that allow for the creation of a new vision (a new person). A doppelgänger of a self, who has the "goal of arriving through its backward journey", as Steve Reinke put it[4]. If you imagine an autobiography that happens in a present moment you'll have to think of it as a piece of automatic writing. Rewriting your life everyday by erasing the past, but the danger behind it is that then there is no life, only art. "What kind of act is to say that life follows art? If it does wouldn't that mean that all facts are products of imagination before they were objectively true?". [5]

I wish this conversation to continue.

4) S. REINKE, *AGAINST AUTOBIOGRAPHY*, HTTP://DEIRDRELOGUE. COM/WRITING/AGAINST_AUTOBIOGRAPHY.HTML
5) M. SAUNDERS, *SELF IMPRESSION: LIFE-WRITING, AUTOBIOGRAFIC-TION, AND THE FORMS OF MODERN LITERATURE*, OXFORD UNIVERSI-TY PRESS, 2010

AFTERWORLDS

AFTERWORD BY MARIUSZ TROJANSKI

An author attempts to find her Self through the prism of the opinions of others. About construction of biography/autobiography as a tool for understanding the Self and everyday practice. At the same time she tries to answer the questions of whether a biography can be treated as a fictional construction or could be understood as a learning process manifested as "life", a performative work. In short, what is biography? And can writing a biography help us understand ourselves?

In her work, she presents various opinions and points of view obtained through interesting discussions with others – writers, psychologists, philosophers, musicians, poets, filmmakers – in the form of e-mail exchanges, never resorting to face to-face conversations. This approach makes her work more remarkable, not only from a psychological point of view but also a sociological one.

REFERENCES

- Ashbery, John. *The System*, In: The Paris Review, No. 53, Winter 1972

- Baker, Nicholson. *U and I: A True Story*; Vintage, 1992

- Brockmeier, Jens. *Autobiographical Time*, In: Bamberg, Michael and Allyssa McCabe, Narrative Identity. Special issue of "Narrative Inquiry" 10:1 (2000). 2000. 265 pp. (pp. 51–73)

- Capek, Karel. *Cross Roads*, Catbird Press, 2002

- Frey, James. *A Million Little Pieces*, Anchor, 2005

- Gazzaniga, Michael S. *Fictional Self*, In: "The Mind's Past", p. 1-28, University of California Press, 2000

- Glowacki, Janusz. *Good Night Dzerzi*, Swiat Ksiazki 2010

- Handke, Peter. *Don Huan: His Own Version*, Farrar, Straus and Giroux, 2011

- Heilbrun, Carolyn (Gold). *Is Biography Fiction?*, In: Soundings: An Interdisciplinary Journal Vol. 76, No. 2/3, Papers from The Drew Symposium (Summer/Fall 1993), pp. 295-314, Penn University Press; Article Stable URL: http://www.jstor.org/stable/41179215

- P. Helguera, *Art Scenes. The Social Scripts of*

the Art World, Jorge Pinto Books Inc., 2012

- Hustvedt, Siri. *The Blazing World*, Simon & Schuster, 2014

- Johnson, B. S. *Albert Angelo*, New Directions, 1987

- Johnson, B. S. *Trawl*, Secker & Warburg, 1966

- Korczynski, Jacob. *I See/La Camera: I*, If I Can't Dance I Don't Want To Be A Part Of Your Revolution, 2014

- Kraus, Chris. *Discuss Rules Beforehand. Ferocity and vulnerability in a posthumously published collection of e-mails from writer/artist/feminist icon Kathy Acker*, In: The Believer, September 2014

- Kraus, Chris. *I Love Dick*, Semiotext(e), 2006

- Lispector, Clarice. *The Hour of the Star*, New Directions, 2011

- McCullers, Carson. *Collected Stories*, Mariner Books, 1998

- Momus, *The Books of Japans*, Solution 214 – 238, Sternberg Press, 2011

- Rollyson, Carl, E. *A Higher Form of Cannibalism? Adventures in the Art and Politics of Biography*, Ivan R. Dee, 2005

- Ruefle, Mary. *On Beginning*, My Emily Dickinson, In: Madness, Rack and Honey: Collected Lectures, Wave Books, 2012

- Saunders, Max. *Self Impression: Life-Writing, Autobiografiction, and the Forms of Modern Literature*, Oxford University Press, 2010

- Shaw, Lytle. *The Moiré Effect*, Cabinet Books & Bookhorse, 2012

- Shields, David. *Reality Hunger: A Manifesto*, Vintage, 2011

- Smith, Martha, Nell. *Rowing in Eden: Rereading Emily Dickinson*, University of Texas Press, 1992

- Sondheim, Alan. *Auto-biography or biog.txt*, http://www.alansondheim.org/biog.txt

- Stein, Gertrude. *The Autobiography of Alice B. Toklas*, Vintage, 1990

- Stephenson, Sam. *Notes from a biographer on W. Eugene Smiths*, In: The Paris Review, https://flipboard.com/section/notes-from-a-biographer-on-w.-eugene-smith-b5JF0G

- Strawson, Galen. *Against Narrativity*, In: Ratio (new series), XVII 4 December 2004

- Strawon, Galen. *The Unstoried Life*, To appear in: "On Life Writing", ed. Z. Leader, Oxford University Press, 2015

- Updike, John. *Self-Consciousness*, Alfred A. Knopf, 1989

INDEX

www.ingramcontent.com/pod-product-compliance
Lightning Source LLC
Chambersburg PA
CBHW072212170526
45158CB00002BA/561